AF228631

MASSACHUSETTS

BY KATE CONLEY

CONTENT CONSULTANT
Robert Forrant, PhD
Distinguished University Professor of History
History Graduate Program Coordinator
University of Massachusetts Lowell

An Imprint of Abdo Publishing
abdobooks.com

abdobooks.com

Published by Abdo Publishing, a division of ABDO, PO Box 398166, Minneapolis, Minnesota 55439. Copyright © 2023 by Abdo Consulting Group, Inc. International copyrights reserved in all countries. No part of this book may be reproduced in any form without written permission from the publisher. Core Library™ is a trademark and logo of Abdo Publishing.

Printed in the United States of America, North Mankato, Minnesota.
052022
092022

Cover Photo: Shutterstock Images, map and icons; HSS Studio/Shutterstock Images, fishing boat
Interior Photos: Sean Pavone/Shutterstock Images, 4–5, 45; Red Line Editorial, 6 (Massachusetts), 6 (USA); Michael Sean O'Leary/Shutterstock Images, 10–11, 13, 20–21, 43; Shutterstock Images, 16 (flag); Gita Kulinitch Studio/Shutterstock Images, 16 (berries); Eve Photography/Shutterstock Images, 16 (dog); Jeff Holcombe/Shutterstock Images, 16 (flower); Michael G. Mill/Shutterstock Images, 16 (bird); Keith J. Finks/Shutterstock Images, 22; MJS Image/Shutterstock Images, 26; JJM Photography/Shutterstock Images, 28–29; Walter Bibikow/DanitaDelimont.com/Danita Delimont Photography/Newscom, 32; Pendleton's Lithography/Library of Congress, 34–35; Steven Senne/AP Images, 39; Denis Tangney Jr./iStockphoto, 40

Editor: Marie Pearson
Series Designer: Joshua Olson

Library of Congress Control Number: 2021951413

Publisher's Cataloging-in-Publication Data

Names: Conley, Kate, author.
Title: Massachusetts / by Kate Conley
Description: Minneapolis, Minnesota : Abdo Publishing, 2023 | Series: Core library of US states | Includes online resources and index.
Identifiers: ISBN 9781532197628 (lib. bdg.) | ISBN 9781098270384 (ebook)
Subjects: LCSH: U.S. states--Juvenile literature. | Northeastern States--Juvenile literature. | Massachusetts--History--Juvenile literature. | Physical geography--United States--Juvenile literature.
Classification: DDC 974.4--dc23

Population demographics broken down by race and ethnicity come from the 2019 census estimate. Population totals come from the 2020 census.

CONTENTS

THE BAY STATE

Hundreds of visitors line up on Boston Common. It is the nation's oldest park. The park is in Boston, Massachusetts. Tour guides greet the visitors. The guides wear costumes from the 1700s. This is a city walking tour. It is also a way to travel back in time to the founding of the United States. The Freedom Trail is a 2.5-mile (4-km) path. It winds through the oldest parts of Boston. Sites include churches, houses, parks, and cemeteries. Each played a role in creating the United States. Few places in the nation

A statue of George Washington stands on Boston Common.

MASSACHUSETTS

Take a look at this map of Massachusetts. How do you think water has been important for the state?

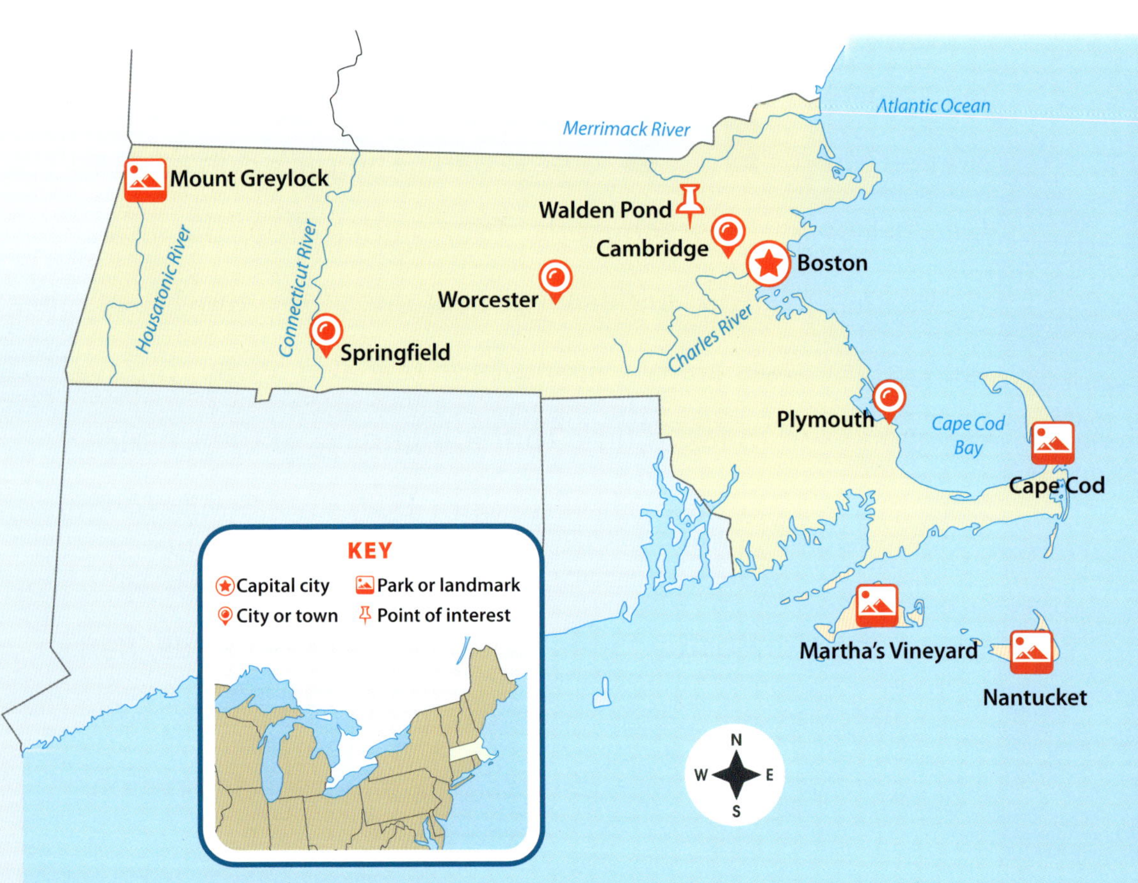

have as many exciting historic sites from the country's early history as Massachusetts.

ABOUT THE STATE

Massachusetts is part of New England. This region is in the northeastern United States. The Atlantic Ocean borders Massachusetts to the east. Vermont and New Hampshire form its northern border. To the south it borders Rhode Island and Connecticut. New York lies along the state's western border.

PERSPECTIVES

THE MASSACHUSETT PEOPLE

Three thousand Massachusett people lived in 20 villages along the coast of present-day Massachusetts when Europeans arrived. War with other nations in the area had greatly hurt the Massachusett people. But that was just the beginning of their troubles. The Europeans exposed the Massachusett people to new diseases such as smallpox. Few Massachusett people survived a smallpox outbreak in 1633. Colonists forced those who survived to give up their homelands and way of life. Today their descendants seek to keep those traditions alive.

The state is named after the Massachusett people. Originally they lived near present-day Massachusetts Bay. They took their name from the name of one of their villages in what is now the Blue Hills. This chain of 22 hills is near Boston. The village was named Massawachusett, meaning "the place of many great hills." Massachusett people continue to live in the state today.

The coast also has many bays. Bays are bodies of water that are partially surrounded by land. Because of its many bays, Massachusetts is often called the Bay State.

HARVARD UNIVERSITY

Colonists founded Harvard University in 1636. Harvard is the oldest college in the United States. It was named after the minister John Harvard. He left his valuable collection of books and a large donation to the school. For most of Harvard's history, only males could attend the school. That changed in the 1960s, when females were allowed to attend. The school boasts many famous graduates, including eight US presidents. Today it is considered one of the top schools in the nation.

Massachusetts is a state with rich history. It remains an important part of the nation. Today Massachusetts is a leader in technology. The state is also known for its excellent schools, including Harvard University. Massachusetts has a lot to offer the nation.

EXPLORE ONLINE

Chapter One describes Boston as a key location in colonial and US history. The interactive map at the website below allows you to explore the city in 1723. What parts of the map surprised you? What are some of the differences between colonial Boston and modern Boston?

EXPLORE COLONIAL BOSTON

abdocorelibrary.com/massachusetts

HISTORY OF MASSACHUSETTS

People have been living in present-day Massachusetts for a long time. Paleo-Indians arrived in the area about 12,000 years ago. Over time, they formed several nations. These include the Massachusett, Wampanoag, Nauset, Pennacook, Nipmuc, and Pocomtuc peoples.

Historians are unsure when Europeans first arrived in the area. Some believe Leif Erikson may have been the first. They think his ship reached what is now Cape Cod around the year 1000 CE. In the 1500s, Europeans

Wampanoag people historically lived in a type of house called a wetu.

began fishing in the waters near Massachusetts. Some Europeans also explored the land. But none of them stayed there permanently.

EUROPEAN SETTLEMENTS

In November 1620 a ship called the *Mayflower* arrived in Cape Cod Bay. It carried 102 passengers from England. They were called the Pilgrims because they were in search of a place to worship freely. The Pilgrims built a settlement near Plymouth. A Wampanoag chief named Massasoit made a peace treaty with them. The two groups lived in peace for many years.

A group of colonists from England arrived in 1630. They were Puritans. Like the Pilgrims, the Puritans wanted religious freedom. They formed the Massachusetts Bay Colony. By 1640 the colony had 16,000 residents. Most had come seeking new opportunities and freedom. But many also wanted to make the Wampanoag people live like white Europeans.

Visitors to Plimoth Patuxet Museums can learn about how the colonists lived at the site in the 1600s.

As the colony grew, so did its problems. Colonists took land from the Wampanoag. Tensions grew. The colonists and American Indians fought in King Philip's War (1675–1676). King Philip was another name for Wampanoag sachem (chief) Metacom. Many Wampanoag villages were destroyed. Colonists settled on the land.

THE AMERICAN REVOLUTION

The colonists grew unhappy with England, the country that ruled the colony. England was in debt from wars. To pay the debt, England's parliament taxed the colonies heavily. This outraged the colonists, who had no one to speak for them in parliament. Many protests, riots, and boycotts took place in Massachusetts. The most famous became known as the Boston Tea Party. Colonists tossed a shipment of tea into the water to protest tea taxes.

The tensions between England and the colonies led to violence. The first battles of the war took place in Massachusetts. Paul Revere and a few other people warned colonists about a planned attack by the British. On April 19, 1775, colonists were waiting for the British troops at the cities of Lexington and Concord. The colonists won. This marked the beginning of the Revolutionary War (1775–1783). Many of the war's battles took place in Massachusetts.

The war lasted until 1783, when the colonists won their freedom. The colonies began to reorganize into states. On February 6, 1788, Massachusetts became the new nation's sixth state.

A GROWING STATE

By the mid-1800s, the country had grown. Tensions were rising between the northern and southern states. The southern states relied on enslaved people to grow crops. Many enslaved people were from Africa or had descended

MASSACHUSETTS
QUICK FACTS

Massachusetts is special to residents for a lot of reasons. How do these facts and symbols help you understand various points of pride for residents?

Abbreviation: MA
Nickname: The Bay State
Motto: *Ense petit placidam sub libertate quietem* (By the sword we seek peace, but peace only under liberty)*
Date of statehood: February 6, 1788
Capital: Boston
Population: 7,029,917
Area: 10,554 square miles (27,335 sq km)

STATE SYMBOLS

State berry
Cranberry

State dog
Boston terrier

State bird
Black-capped chickadee

State flower
Mayflower (trailing arbutus)

*Beginning in 2021, a commission was created with the goal to recommend changes to the flag and motto. The current state symbols have been criticized as being disrespectful to American Indians.

from enslaved Africans. In the northern states, many people believed slavery should be illegal. The two sides fought in the American Civil War (1861–1865).

Massachusetts and other northern states formed the Union. Nearly 160,000 men from Massachusetts fought for the Union. Massachusetts also created one of the nation's first military units of Black soldiers. It was called the Fifty-Fourth Massachusetts. More than 1,000 men volunteered for the unit. They were known for their bravery in battle. The Union won the war, and slavery was made illegal in the country.

After the war's end, many factories and fisheries opened or expanded in the state. These provided new jobs, which drew many workers, including immigrants. They settled in places such as Fall River, New Bedford, Holyoke, Worcester, Lowell, and Lawrence. By 1930 approximately 65 percent of people in Massachusetts were foreign born or had at least one foreign-born parent.

Today the state government is made of the legislative, executive, and judicial branches. Members of the Senate and House of Representatives in the legislative branch write bills. In the executive branch, the governor can sign bills into law. And the judicial branch, which contains the courts, applies the law to court cases. Massachusetts is a far different place than when the Pilgrims arrived. But many of the values of freedom and industry remain the same.

In 1775 Paul Revere wrote an account of his famous ride. In it he described his actions once he had the warning to deliver:

> *I sett off, it was then about 11 oClock, the Moon shone bright. I had got almost over Charlestown Common, towards Cambridge, when I saw two [British] Officers on Horse-back, standing under the shade of a Tree, in a narrow part of the roade. . . . One of them Star-ted his horse towards me, the other up the road, as I supposed, to head me should I escape the first. I turned my horse short, about, and rid upon a full Gallop for Mistick Road, he followed me about 300 Yardes [270 m], and finding He could not catch me, returned: I proceeded to Lexington.*
>
> *Source: "Paul Revere's Deposition, Fair Copy, circa 1775." Massachusetts Historical Society, n.d., masshist.org. Accessed 22 June 2021.*

CONSIDER YOUR AUDIENCE

Adapt this passage for a different audience, such as your friends. Write a blog post conveying this same information to the new audience. How does your post differ from the original text and why?

GEOGRAPHY AND CLIMATE

Massachusetts has a variety of landscapes. The east side of the state borders the Atlantic Ocean. The coastline stretches for 1,500 miles (2,400 km). Land along the coast varies from rocky bluffs to sandy beaches. There are islands offshore. Two of the largest islands are Martha's Vineyard and Nantucket. They are popular vacation spots. A large peninsula called Cape Cod extends into the ocean. This long, narrow piece of land has a distinctive hook shape.

The Nobska Light is a popular Cape Cod landmark.

Central Massachusetts has rolling plains. The plains gradually give way to the Berkshire Hills in the western part of the state. These hills are part of the Appalachian Mountains. The Berkshires are known for their peaceful woods, rivers, and trails. The state's highest point, Mount Greylock, is in the Berkshires. It is 3,491 feet (1,064 m) tall.

Massachusetts is also rich in waterways. Rivers wind their way across the state and flow into the Atlantic Ocean. The state's main rivers are the Connecticut, the Housatonic, the Merrimack, and the Charles Rivers. The Charles River is the longest river within the state.

It starts in Hopkinton and winds its way for 80 miles (130 km) until it reaches Boston Harbor. In addition to rivers, the state also has more than 3,000 lakes and ponds.

CLIMATE

The climate in Massachusetts is temperate. It has four distinct seasons. The winter is cold, with average temperatures around 32 degrees Fahrenheit (0°C). Winter storms are called northeasters, or nor'easters. They form

WALDEN POND

One of the most famous bodies of water in Massachusetts is Walden Pond. It became well known through Henry David Thoreau. He was a writer and naturalist. In July 1845 he moved into a cabin he built on Walden Pond. He lived there alone in the wilderness, writing about his experiences. Thoreau later wrote a book called *Walden*. It has become an American classic on how people can live more closely connected to nature. Today Walden Pond is a national historic landmark.

off the coast between October and April. Nor'easters can bring sleet, several feet of snow, and high winds. Sometimes the winds are so strong they create blizzards.

The warmer temperatures of spring melt the snow. Spring then gives way to hot summers. The average summer temperature is 80 degrees Fahrenheit (26°C). Many people enjoy going to the state's lakes, beaches, and islands to cool off during these months. The summer can also bring thunderstorms.

Fall is brisk and cool. It also is when the state's many trees put on an impressive display. Their leaves go from green to shades of yellow, orange, brown, gold, and red in September and October. Tourists come from across the nation to view them.

PLANTS AND ANIMALS

Massachusetts is densely populated. But it has managed to keep many areas natural. About 60 percent of the state is covered in forests. The most common trees in these forests are white pine, red maple, northern red oak, and hemlock. In spring, the pink or white buds of the Mayflower plant bloom.

The forests of Massachusetts provide a habitat for many animals. Large wild animals such as black bears, bobcats, coyotes, moose, and deer all live in the forests. Smaller animals live there too. These include beavers, river otters, opossums, turkeys, raccoons, and black-capped chickadees.

Great blue herons are one of many bird species that live in Massachusetts. They grow to about 4 feet (1.2 m) tall.

Along the coastal areas, plants and animals are different. Sand dunes on the coast are home to a variety of native grasses. These plants can tolerate high winds, salt spray from the ocean, and flooding. The waters along the coast are rich in sea life. This includes many types of fish. Birds such as sandpipers, herons, and egrets soar over the coastal waters.

SOURCE

Massachusetts is full of beautiful locations, including cities. Lucas Ferreira attended college in Massachusetts in 2016. He explained some of the things he loved about the state:

> *While there are way too many interesting and beautiful nooks and crannies to count in Massachusetts, the North Shore (especially around Gloucester and Newburyport) is just way too pretty to ever pass up. . . . So far I've explored both the North and South coast of Boston to a decent extent, and I can't remember ever being visually disappointed with some of the cities I've seen. This is where the history part comes back too, because really if you pay close enough attention there are some awesome things to see that every city offers.*
>
> *Source: Lucas Ferreira. "10 Reasons Why I Love Massachusetts." Odyssey, 10 Oct. 2016, theodysseyonline.com. Accessed 8 July 2021.*

BACK IT UP

The author of this passage is using evidence to support a point. Write a paragraph describing the point the author is making. Then write down two or three pieces of evidence the author uses to make the point.

RESOURCES AND ECONOMY

The Atlantic Ocean has played a large role in the economy of Massachusetts. It's one of the state's largest natural resources. Early European settlers relied on it to strengthen the colony's economy. They built boats and fished for cod off the coast. Then the colonists salted the cod to preserve it and traded it for goods with the British. Over time, trade expanded to other parts of Europe and the West Indies.

Dry Dock 1 in Boston has been used to repair ships since 1833.

Today fishing is still an important industry in Massachusetts.

Building ships has been an important part of the state's economy for a long time. Colonists in Massachusetts built the first ship in 1631. Boston and other coastal towns quickly became industry leaders. During the 1700s Massachusetts was the main supplier of ships to the other colonies. It remained an important part of the state's economy until the 1960s.

MANUFACTURING

Since the 1800s, Massachusetts has been a leader in manufacturing. Francis Cabot Lowell opened a textile factory in Waltham in 1814. His factory used new technology to make the operation efficient. Workers processed raw cotton, spun it into thread, and wove it into finished cloth. They did all the work in one building. This had never been done before. The process made cloth cheaper and faster to produce.

Lowell hired local, unmarried women. They lived in boarding houses owned and operated by the factory owners. A woman called a matron watched over the women to make sure they behaved. The factory jobs provided opportunities for women to earn money. It gained them new freedoms away from their families. But the jobs were dangerous. The women worked in harsh conditions for long hours.

Despite these problems, the Lowell system caught on quickly. It allowed goods to be produced at a low

cost in a short time. Other manufacturers in the state began to model their factories on Lowell's. By 1900 half of all the shoes and boots made in the nation came from factories in Massachusetts. Factories in the state also made shovels, guns, envelopes, and other goods.

NEW INDUSTRIES

Gradually new industries took over. Today health care is the largest industry in the state. It employs approximately 300,000 people. They work in hospitals, clinics, and care facilities. The state is home to Brigham and Women's Hospital and Massachusetts General Hospital. They are two of the nation's largest hospitals.

And many health-care workers study at the University of Massachusetts Medical School in Worcester.

The service industry is also important to the economy in Massachusetts. The state's colleges and universities employ thousands of residents. Restaurants, hotels, and shops cater to the many tourists who visit the state each year. Massachusetts is also home to financial companies that provide services to clients across the nation. Technology research, development, and manufacturing are other important industries in the state.

PEOPLE AND PLACES

Throughout the state's history, the people of Massachusetts have contributed to the nation. Three presidents were born and raised there. They are John Adams, John Quincy Adams, and John F. Kennedy.

The state has also produced many beloved writers. Louisa May Alcott, the author of *Little Women*, spent most of her life in Boston. Poet Henry Wadsworth Longfellow lived in Cambridge for more than 40 years. Writer Nathaniel Hawthorne also lived in the state.

John Adams was the second US president. He served from 1797 to 1801.

He set his two most famous novels, *The Scarlet Letter* and *The House of the Seven Gables*, in his home state.

POPULATION

There are more than 7 million people in Massachusetts. White people who are not Hispanic or Latino make up 71 percent of the population. The next largest groups are Hispanic and Latino people at 12 percent and Black people at 9 percent. Asian people make up 7 percent. Massachusetts also has two federally recognized American Indian tribes. They are the Mashpee Wampanoag Tribe and the

Wampanoag Tribe of
Gay Head (Aquinnah).

Many people in
Massachusetts descend
from immigrants. The
earliest European
settlers came from
England. But later
they began to arrive
from other places
in Europe. Between
1820 and 1930,
4.5 million immigrants
from Ireland arrived
in the United States.
Many of them settled
in Massachusetts,
particularly Boston.
In 2019 more than
1.3 million people in

IRISH NEED NOT APPLY

When the Irish immigrants arrived in Massachusetts in great numbers, they often faced difficulties. Many came to the United States to escape from a famine in Ireland. Most were unskilled and Catholic. They had little money. Some people grew suspicious of the new immigrants. The Irish faced discrimination. Job ads often stated, "Irish need not apply." Catholic churches were burned by anti-Irish mobs. Some people believed the stereotype that the Irish were violent and drank too much alcohol. The discrimination lasted for many years. But today the descendants of Irish immigrants have become leaders in all areas of the nation.

Massachusetts had Irish roots. It is the state's largest ethnic group.

Immigrants and refugees from around the world continue to arrive in Massachusetts. They are adding their own cultures and traditions to the state. Since the 1980s the largest numbers of immigrants have come to the state from Brazil, China, India, and the Dominican Republic. Many people also come from Southeast Asia. In 2019 Massachusetts ranked seventh in the nation for foreign-born residents.

PLACES

The cities in Massachusetts offer many activities. Boston is the state's capital and the largest city, with a population of 675,647. The city is bursting with historic neighborhoods and buildings. Many tourists visit these sites to learn about life in the past. For example, the Black Heritage Trail includes several sites that were part of a historically Black community. People here helped Black people escape from slavery and also fought for

The team that would become the Boston Red Sox was founded in 1901.

equal rights. But Boston is also modern. It has new theaters, restaurants, shops, and homes. It also has professional sports teams such as the Red Sox, the Celtics, and the Bruins.

Worcester is west of Boston. It is located on the Blackstone River and is the state's second-largest city. Like Boston, it has many historical sites. It was

The Basketball Hall of Fame's latest building opened in 2002.

an important stop on the Underground Railroad. The Worcester Music Festival began there in 1858. It still provides concertgoers with music every year, making it the nation's oldest music festival.

West of Worcester is the city of Springfield. In the 1800s, it became an important industrial town, producing paper, train cars, and ice skates. Athlete James Naismith invented the game of basketball in Springfield in 1891. The Basketball Hall of Fame is located there in his honor.

The people of Massachusetts are proud of their state. It played a key role in the nation's early history. Its people helped win independence from England. And people continue to move to the state. Today Massachusetts is a state filled with diversity and talent.

FURTHER EVIDENCE

Chapter Five discusses the people who make up the state of Massachusetts. What is the main point of the chapter? What key evidence supports this point? Go to the website below about immigrants in Massachusetts. Find a quote from the website that supports the chapter's main theme.

ETHNIC GROUPS

abdocorelibrary.com/massachusetts

IMPORTANT DATES

10,000 BCE

Paleo-Indians arrive in present-day Massachusetts as the area's first settlers.

1620

Pilgrims aboard the *Mayflower* arrive in present-day Massachusetts. They establish a village and are on friendly terms with the Wampanoag people.

1630

Puritans establish the Massachusetts Bay Colony. The colony quickly grows.

1775–1783

The Revolutionary War takes place. It begins in Lexington and Concord in Massachusetts. Many other battles throughout the war take place in the state.

1788

Massachusetts becomes a state on February 6, making it the sixth in the new nation.

1820–1930

A large wave of immigrants from Ireland comes to Massachusetts. The immigrants face discrimination and hatred for many years.

1861–1865

Massachusetts takes part in the American Civil War, fighting on the site of the Union. It sends one of the nation's first Black military units to fight.

2019

Massachusetts ranks seventh in the nation for foreign-born residents.

Say What?

Studying a state and its history can mean learning a lot of new vocabulary. Find five words in this book you've never heard before. Use a dictionary to find out what they mean. Then write the meanings in your own words and use each word in a new sentence.

Take a Stand

Massachusetts has a variety of landscapes, from coastal beaches to inland hills. Which area do you think would be most interesting to visit? Write a paragraph explaining why that region would be at the top of your list.

Dig Deeper

After reading this book, what questions do you still have about Massachusetts? With an adult's help, find a few reliable sources that can help you answer your questions. Write a paragraph about what you learned.

Another View

Chapter Two talks about King Philip's War. As you know, every source is different. Ask a librarian or another adult to help you find another source about this topic. Write a short essay comparing and contrasting the new source's point of view with that of this book's author. What is the point of view of each author? How are they similar and why? How are they different and why?

GLOSSARY

boycott
the act of avoiding dealing with someone or something in order to make a change

discrimination
when people treat others differently based on certain factors such as appearance

dune
a mound of sand formed by the wind

enlist
to sign up

ethnic
relating to a group that shares a common background and culture

naturalist
a person who studies nature

parliament
a group of people who make laws for a country

peninsula
a body of land that is surrounded by water on three sides

sewage
human waste

temperate
a climate that does not have extremely hot or cold temperatures

ONLINE RESOURCES

To learn more about Massachusetts, visit our free resource websites below.

Visit **abdocorelibrary.com** or scan this QR code for free Common Core resources for teachers and students, including vetted activities, multimedia, and booklinks, for deeper subject comprehension.

Visit **abdobooklinks.com** or scan this QR code for free additional online weblinks for further learning. These links are routinely monitored and updated to provide the most current information available.

LEARN MORE

Elston, Heidi M. D. *John Adams.* Abdo, 2021.

Harris, Duchess. *The Boston Tea Party.* Abdo, 2018.

Messner, Kate. *The Mayflower.* Random House, 2020.

INDEX

About the Author

Kate Conley has been writing nonfiction books for children for more than ten years. When she's not writing, Conley spends her time reading, sewing, and solving crossword puzzles. She lives in Minnesota with her husband and two children.